Letters to:

From:

Date begun:

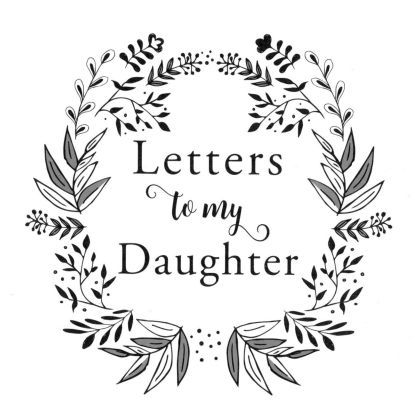

# Letters to my Daughter

With love from:

..........................................................................

P

PETER PAUPER PRESS, INC.
WHITE PLAINS, NEW YORK

## PETER PAUPER PRESS

In 1928, at the age of twenty-two, Peter Beilenson began printing books on a small press in the basement of his parents' home in Larchmont, New York. Peter—and later, his wife, Edna—sought to create fine books that sold at "prices even a pauper could afford."

Today, still family owned and operated, Peter Pauper Press continues to honor our founders' legacy—and customers' expectations—of beauty, quality, and value.

Copyright © 2020
Peter Pauper Press, Inc.
202 Mamaroneck Avenue
White Plains, NY 10601 USA
All rights reserved
ISBN 978-1-4413-3413-8
Printed in China

7 6 5

Visit us at www.peterpauper.com

# Dear Parent,

So many thoughts and emotions revolve around our experiences with our children, from bits of wisdom to feelings of love or concern. Here's the place to record all of these, as well as hopes and memories.

Begin when they're newborn, or pick up when they're teenagers. Use this as your private journal, or create a keepsake to share.

XOXO

Date:

Date:

Date:

Date:

Date:

Date:

Date:

Date:

Just a note:

Date:

Just a note:

Date:

*Just a note*:

Date:

---

*Just a note*:

Date:

Date:

Date:

Date:

Date:

Date:

Date:

Date:

Date:

*Just a note*:

Date:

---

*Just a note*:

Date:

*Just a note:*

Date:

---

*Just a note:*

Date:

Date:

Date:

Date:

Date:

Date:

Date:

Date:

Date:

*Just a note:*

Date:

---

*Just a note:*

Date:

*Just a note*:

Date: ................................

.................................................................................

.................................................................................

.................................................................................

.................................................................................

.................................................................................

.................................................................................

*Just a note*:

Date: ................................

.................................................................................

.................................................................................

.................................................................................

.................................................................................

.................................................................................

.................................................................................

Date:

Date:

Date:

Date:

Date:

**Date:**

Date:

Date:

*Just a note:*

Date:

---

*Just a note:*

Date:

*Just a note:*

Date: ......................................

..........................................................................................................

..........................................................................................................

..........................................................................................................

..........................................................................................................

..........................................................................................................

..........................................................................................................

..........................................................................................................


*Just a note:*

Date: ......................................

..........................................................................................................

..........................................................................................................

..........................................................................................................

..........................................................................................................

..........................................................................................................

..........................................................................................................

..........................................................................................................

Date:

Date:

Date:

Date:

Date:

Date:

Date:

Date:

_Just a note:_

Date:

---

_Just a note:_

Date:

*Just a note:*

Date: .....................

*Just a note:*

Date: .....................

Date:

Date:

Date:

Date:

Date:

Date:

Date:

Date:

*Just a note:*

Date: ........................

_____

_____

_____

_____

_____

_____

_____


*Just a note:*

Date: ........................

_____

_____

_____

_____

_____

_____

_____

## Just a note:

Date:

## Just a note:

Date:

Date:

Date:

Date:

Date:

Date:

Date: ................................

Date:

Date:

*Just a note:*

Date:

---

*Just a note:*

Date:

*Just a note:*

Date:

---

*Just a note:*

Date:

Date:

Date:

Date:

Date:

Date:

Date:

Date:

Date:

*Just a note:*

Date: .......................................

........................................................................................................

........................................................................................................

........................................................................................................

........................................................................................................

........................................................................................................

........................................................................................................

........................................................................................................


*Just a note:*

Date: .......................................

........................................................................................................

........................................................................................................

........................................................................................................

........................................................................................................

........................................................................................................

........................................................................................................

........................................................................................................

*Just a note:*

Date: ......................

---

*Just a note:*

Date: ......................

Date:

Date:

Date:

Date: .........................................

Date:

Date:

Date:

Date:

_Just a note:_

Date:

---

_Just a note:_

Date:

*Just a note*:

Date: ................................

.................................................................................................................

.................................................................................................................

.................................................................................................................

.................................................................................................................

.................................................................................................................

.................................................................................................................

.................................................................................................................

.................................................................................................................


*Just a note*:

Date: ................................

.................................................................................................................

.................................................................................................................

.................................................................................................................

.................................................................................................................

.................................................................................................................

.................................................................................................................

.................................................................................................................

Date:

Date:

Date:

Date:

Date:

Date:

Date:

Date:

*Just a note:*

Date:

---

*Just a note:*

Date:

*Just a note*:

Date:

---

*Just a note*:

Date:

Date:

Date:

Date:

Date:

Date:

Date:

Date:

Date: ........................................

Date: